This *Way* the Road

This *Way* the Road

NINA BERKHOUT

NEWEST PRESS

Library and Archives Canada Cataloguing in Publication
Berkhout, Nina, 1975-
This way the road / Nina Berkhout.

Poems.
ISBN 1-896300-92-8

I. Title.

PS8553.E688T48 2005   C811'.6   C2005-903530-7

Board editor: Don Kerr
Cover and interior design: Ruth Linka
Cover images: istockphoto.com
Author photo: Denise Ouellette-Berkhout

 Canada Council   Conseil des Arts
for the Arts   du Canada   Canadian Patrimoine   edmonton
Heritage   canadien   arts
council

NeWest Press acknowledges the support of the Canada Council for the Arts
and the Alberta Foundation for the Arts, and the Edmonton Arts Council
for our publishing program. We also acknowledge the financial support
of the Government of Canada through the Book Publishing Industry
Development Program (BPIDP) for our publishing activities.

NeWest Press
201–8540–109 Street
Edmonton, Alberta T6G 1E6
(780) 432-9427
www.newestpress.com

NeWest Press is committed to protecting the environment and to the responsible use of
natural resources. This book is printed on 100% post-consumer recycled and ancient-for-
est-friendly paper. For more information please visit www.oldgrowthfree.com.

1 2 3 4 5 08 07 06 05

PRINTED AND BOUND IN CANADA

marms, pater, sis
up
lifting

Contents

Ascension ✤ I

Flamebirds ✤ 37

Into Thin Air ✤ 75

✤ ✤ ✤

I boarded the king's ship; now in the beak,
now in the waist, the deck, in every cabin,
I flamed in amazement; sometimes I'd divide
and burn in many places; on the topmast
the yards and bowsprit, would I flame distinctly
then meet and join.

William Shakespeare, *The Tempest*, Act I, Scene 2

✤ ✤ ✤

�֍ I �֍

Ascension

Down comes what
went up

✣

A glass artifact falls from scaffolding.

Crashing onto the floor
like a thousand windchimes cracking,

tumbling a nightingale at my feet.

Over your head there were always chandeliers.
In cafes and restaurants, bars and hallways, crystal
spiders dangling

in the bistro up there gleaming, suspended
from a gilt ceiling above me

waiting
as usual, in my best crimson dress.

Come now winter, fang me
white.

Love lopes through our galleries
spade tongue darting

✤

During the ice storm, I told Anna I loved Jules.
We were trapped in her studio.

Crouching near the oven, my hands
grazing across glass shavings
on the concrete floor, slivers

invisible and sharp in my skin.

Convinced death was Anna's latest masterpiece
(a lifesize Medusa watching from the catwalk), I confessed:

— I love the one in the studio next to you
— you mean the guy who makes white blobs?
— it's called *layering* Anna
— Christ, couldn't he be more creative besides he's rude never says hello
— maybe he's shy
— Helen does this jerk even know you exist?
— not yet his name is Jules

Electricity returns: flickering lights drain the storm blue
from Anna's sculptures, we hear a steel door
slamming it's Anna's professor lover
come to the rescue.

Midwinter bleeds
snow

✤

What was it about this man
wasn't first sight love I'd never
laid eyes on him

when some pang struck my throat,
yanking at my neck roots.

Once Upon a Time I burned beside Anna's kiln
while she spun snakes for Medusa's hair:
into the fire, then out to twist serpentines,
then into the oven again.

Sudden came the throat snag,
Anna said *what's wrong have you seen a ghost*
as I stared into her heat machine then up at walls
where red globules danced everywhere.

Boiling Point: pulse quickening I blinked hard,
left her studio to cool off, turned a corner

There He Was
shining at the back of the room

in toque and trench coat, on a ladder dipping
his hands in a bucket, smoothing white paint
onto an immense iceberg.

One day I'd like to go north, smiled blue eyes.

Icing on the cake:
that night on CBC I heard the *fulgurite* phenomenon:
brittle, glassy formations shivering
in a wide open plane: lightning striking sandy soil
Eureka.

Caught in the spined trap
of your legs

❧

Walk with me through my museum,
this is where he finds me hesitating
between gallery spaces.

To reach my office I can turn left or right:
through the gallery on the left
I pass beneath the albatross
suspended by wires behind a vitrine,

stiff from carrying countless souls of mariners
back and forth across the sea

when sailors saw an albatross
it meant bad storms or fog ahead, says my label,
if they harmed or killed the bird, it was worse luck.

In this gallery, I tread upon
antarctic nests of small stones.

Turn right. Here, Phaeton fades
like a spectre from a kalyx crater, adolescent
falling from constellations,

his father's chariot burning
him down. Phaeton brings to mind Anna's nephew
who borrowed Anna's brother's car last year

then died in fire.

Even so, the albatross' stare
has me heading for the Phaeton room and this
is where he finds me, my lover

emerging from the corridor
like a long, ivory
tooth.

Code orange in
Cloudland

✢

Phaeton's label goes like this:

(Jules is walking toward me now)

Phaeton was son of sun god Helios and nymph Clymene.
When a classmate howled at the notion of his being son of a deity,
Phaeton ran enraged to his mother

hi my name is Jules, I work next to Anna do you remember me

"if I'm of heavenly birth mom, prove it!" he hollered.
Clymene told him to go see for himself and demand of Helios
to confess. So Phaeton traveled to India's sunrise
until he reached his father, glittering like a diamond on his throne.

she told me you could provide me with information on roman glass

Laying aside his beams, Helios said, "my boy, to end your doubts,
I'll give you whatever you want." Phaeton immediately asked
to drive his father's chariot.

I'm trying to coat a perfume bottle

Too late, Helios realized his mistake— "Listen, I've spoken too soon,
you ask what's beyond a mortal's power you'll get too dizzy
you'll never keep course and my horses have breasts full of fire
they're nasty creatures don't go son, let's drink ambrosia instead."

so can you tell me if the flask would survive the weight of two thousand layers

Ignoring his father, young Phaeton leapt onto the golden chariot.
Dawn threw open the East's doors, the Day-star ordered glow specs to vanish
and the steeds arrived bloated with nectar . . . "stay in the middle avoid north
and south, one last chance to change your mind boy . . ."

I'll call this sculpture Masking Scenturies

But Phaeton has already grasped the reins, laughing, he's off.
Cloud-cleaving horses spring forward, outrunning morning.
Their load is lighter than usual, the chariot smashes about
like a ship beneath the albatross, tossed against the sea.

so how long have you worked here Anna says you write exhibit text

The horses leave the traveled road, galloping headlong
through bristly groves, hurling over pathlessness.
Constellations flee. The great and little bear are scorched, serpent
coils round the north pole.

do you ever rewrite history nice cameo brooch by the way

Phaeton's eyes grow dim from the glare surrounding him,
he forgets the names of the steeds and fireballs
toward the scorpion's crooked arms, reins falling from his hands.

say your friend Anna's not much of a talker is she

Mountain tops flame, plants wither, fountains run dry, cities perish.
Mortals and minor deities are consumed to ashes.

some of the guys say she's got glass up her ass but I defend her

Phaeton beholds a burning world and can't take the heat.
The air he breathes is hotter than Hades, disheveled nymphs
mourn their lakes, Nile hides in the desert, the sea
withers up, dolphins gone.

anyway thanks for your help, better get back to work but before I go,

The child on fire
falls headlong, marking the heavens with brightness
before burning out in a river.

I hope this isn't too forward but would you mind

Phaeton's sisters weep until they're turned into poplars,
tears hardening to pebbles in a stream.

if I call you?

From now on we fall from sky

✤

A staff meeting is announced.

Hundreds shuffle from storage rooms and vaults,
assembling beneath the aluminum Phoenix sculpture
that hangs from a golden dome.

"This year we need a real hit, a blockbuster
to draw in the crowds no more mummies or dinosaurs
or Syrian gold no that won't do anymore need something

sensational
bigger than the Titanic bigger even than those towers just as
tragic back then, the LZ 129 you all know what I'm referring to,

the Hindenburg!

and I'm counting on YOU (finger arrowing audience),
dedicated staff (leans into microphone yelling louder),
to make our show a blazing success" (smile, bow, exit
Museum Director).

Pulling on my tendons
as if cables of a hot air balloon

✣

Didn't take long he was no common bird
no one night stand no jet of exhaust rapidly evaporating

Jules Murano was no paper cut healing within the hour

couldn't drift away like a bored balloon
as I did with other lovers, he embedded himself

in my veins like a sand spec landing in molten glass
before it solidifies.

In the world's tallest tower we ate dinner in the clouds—
on a glass floor looking 1,465 feet down, he spun me
round then said *let's live together.*

No place for vertigo in Jules' lazuline gaze.

Took me home that night, layered my hip bone white
till it hardened to a cast
jutting out like the seagull's wing.

Preparing another
still life

✣

He only paints white

until the object beneath solidifies to a ghostly (ghostly
says Anna, why not just papier mâché) form
Jules continues layering into the thousands

what's inside, I ask him
and sometimes the label says so or not
depending on Jules' mood.

He calls his sculptures My Capsules.
One night I found him coating his left arm,

the gallery presenting his ghosts
had gone bankrupt
(would have been his New York debut, titled
Murano: Unlayered)

Jules slumped in a closet coating himself pale,
mourning the millions of skins on his sculptures,
muttering
sinistra manu, sinistra manu:

sinister (left)   hand.

The albatross glides above soundlessly

꙳

The phoenix frame crumples onto the mosaic floor.

Sun cuts through the museum's stained glass
setting the silver heap ablaze.

The aluminum sculpture is replaced with another skeleton,
this time layered in silk and hanged
from the dome where scripture warns

That All Men May Know His Work.

Everyone entering my museum now
must pass beneath the Hindenburg airship.

Our magnolia tree is in bloom.
Pale pink claws reach upward then open.

&

The spring I move into Jules' apartment,
Anna housewarms me with a millefiori paperweight.

She holds the glass ball to her eye like a monocle,
staring at Jules' corner of deformities:

ivory rosary (Grandmother Murano's)
coin (loon)
letter (victorian valentine, used bookstore: Dearest D. O. , I-)
fingernail clipping (mine)
umbrella (white. opened)
umbrella (black. closed)
cameo brooch (my great-grandmother's, Jules took the brooch without asking)
compact disc: Górecki (mine again why don't you start coating your own
        stuff Jules?)
stuffed bald eagle (Grandfather Murano's taxidermy shop)
hair (mine, first grey strand)
little fried halo (Galaxy Donut Shop)
braille poem (T. S. Eliot Ash
Wednesday)

— so what's he doing in Montreal?
— a show called Scraps, sculptures from bits of paper found on the
        ground
— that's it white blobs over dirty paper?
— words from love letters, like "you never (torn)" and "how could (torn)"
        and " this way -(torn)"

— how profound
— shutup let's go for a walk

touring the neighbourhood we pass the asylum
and head for Garbage Kingdom antiques,
drawn to the window by a lampshade swept with feathers

— a ripoff if you ask me Helen, why not just pluck that albatross in your
museum it'd be cheaper and why'd you guys have to live near 999,
it's bad karma.

Anna leaves for her studio,
I march home cradling my new lamp.

Next day Jules returns, sees feathers and light
says I'll burn the apartment down did
an asylum patient give me this thing?

Burn these canary
eyes singing so loud

✤

To reach the asylum turn right onto Queen Street,
pass the old candy factory converted into lofts
where glass columns filled with sweets

support a bubblegum-pink building.
Next door, wisteria droops and clings to the walls
built by patients themselves.

Young upper class professionals stride down the sidewalk
(never on the asylum side)—
film and fashion crews darting into bistros, martini bars,
designer clothing shops.

Sundays, Anna and I meet across from 999
at Bar None.

In this cold metal room we smoke Gitanes and drink
La Fin Du Monde beer watching crazies limp past,
most of whom I've grown fond of

— Jesus did you get a look at that one?
— that's the Man in White
— his name for himself or yours?
— mine he always wears white, white windbreaker even in summer,
white turban white shoes socks pants shirt white laundry bag full of
soiled whiteness but look inside the little white cricket cage he carries, tell
me what you see

— bet he can't wait for his beard to turn white, a canary?
— yep, by the way what
do you know about the Hindenburg it's my next project
— who?

Curator's scrawl hissing like a steam burn

⁘

Need to start brainstorming Helen, read my notes tell me
what you think.

Page One let us examine the Disaster:

> • Captured on film for world to see
> • Evil personified: Hitler's propaganda machine

(Helen please insert headlines from May 7, 1936
ie. New York Times: "Airship like a giant torch" & "Germany shocked by
  the tragedy"
& Akron Beach Journal "It might have been an enemy plot").

> • Explosion: dull thump sound like a gas stove lighting
> • People blown from windows falling like snow
> • Air that day clouded like sound through
>   a torn eardrum
> • Airships as weapons (Zeppelins as WWI bombers),
>   approaching target silently from above
> • Steel scraps from wreckage used as WWII weaponry,
>   melted then reforged into frames for German fighter aircraft
> • 804 feet long, almost as tall as Eiffel Tower: gigantic for 1930s,
>   with observation deck and babygrand
> • Luxurious and seemingly safe, also
>   flammable

* Helen note May 6th 2005 as 69th anniversary of disaster, Naval
air engineering station tours every second Saturday (foreign
nationals not allowed since September 2001).

Cooling
temperatures

✦

Anna, you there? Pick up Anna, you there? Need to talk
came home to Jules with a blood red forehead
said he hit it on the corner of the medicine cabinet
but the corners have rubber on them Anna
he wouldn't tell me what happened
only asked for ice kept mumbling get me more ice cubes
made me go out and buy bags of it, thought
he wanted to have a party so I went
but Anna he filled the tub with ice, sat in there for hours
came out blue wouldn't talk to me
don't know what's got into him, you there Anna?
Pick up, call me back.

Don't tell me you were layering

✤

— Forehead better today?
— much, what's this?
— gift. Chandelier pear, asked Anna to make it
to remind you of Bar None's fruit chandelier hanging
above our favourite table, know the one I'm talking about?
— chandelier in there? never noticed
— you can't coat this one it's for the windowsill
— let's get married
— c'mon don't kid around
— who's kidding lemme take you to the arctic
— Jules I hate the cold, bad circulation you know that,
why this obsession with all things north?
— cold preserves, time won't pass we won't-
— Just take your goddamn pear and tell me
where were you last night till 4 AM?

Paper eats away at itself
I am digging through museum archives

✤

Senility is my neighbour. Today
I avoid the zeppelin text to investigate my
asylum.

In a pile of newspapers yellower than
old smoker's teeth, I find headlining news:

In 1853, the doors of the third largest
in North America, named Provincial Lunatic Asylum,
open

in empty green fields east of Parkdale,
remote enough from society to be properly
     admired

bad boys and girls living in Toronto are warned:
"you'll end up in 999" or,
"we'll take you to 666," upside-down mark
of the beast.

Nine Ninety Nine Queen Street West—

Nuthouse madhouse loony bin.
Before the asylum abnormal behaviours
were equated with demonic possession,

treatment included beating whipping execution or
rounding up by sailors for exile.

A new term is born: "ship of fools."

Anna in her studio, blowing technicolour bulbs

✤

— Anna, he has bath salts from the Dead Sea. Tells me my face
is a totem changing each time he sees me says it's uncanny
like weather, tells me he relies on my voice
like a piece of cloud
— uhuh. Read the recipe, will you?
— for clear glass add manganese. Increase the dosage, arrive
at purple. To create blue add cobalt, for red add gold
dust. Copper forms turquoise, pale blue and dark green hues
while antimony turns glass pale orange. For yellow add silver, for white
add tin add too much of any color or chemical, the result will be
black glass
— thanks, think I'm done for tonight let's get a drink. You know,
Helen, a free-floating iceberg isn't stable. Fact is, bergs flip
without warning. Saw it on National Geographic.

Curator's Scrawl: brought about by discharges of an electrostatic nature

❀

Helen please create a module
on the three crash theories here they are:

Number One Weather
Maybe lightning. Or accidental sparks
of electrostatic discharge called Erasmus' Fire
aka Spook Lights, Corposant, Jack-o'-Lantern,

Saint Elmo's Fire:

named for the saint martyred by having his intestines
wound around a capstan.

During thunderstorms, air between clouds and ground
becomes electrically charged, emitting a blue-green glow
along the extremities of tall objects such as treetops, airplane wings,
church spires, sailing masts.

Elmo became patron saint of sailors. During rough weather,
frightened seamen interpreted masthead luminosity
as a sign of his protection.

Witnesses saw a pink radiance inside the hull
and a dim curacao flame licking
the airship's back.

So the ship was enveloped in a glowing electric halo,
pretty theory.

Number Two Sabotage
Bomb along the catwalk in lift cell number four.
Result: loose piece of airship skin flapping in the wind,
a vision of Saint Elmo then hydrogen
in sixteen lift cells burning.

Suspect #1: American comic acrobat Joseph Spah,
who brought a dog back from Germany for his children
and who often snuck into the bowels of the ship
to visit the puppy.

Suspect #2: Eric Spehl, introverted German crewman
with anti-nazi friends, who died in the explosion

(FBI found no conclusive evidence
against Spah or Spehl).

Number Three Design Flaw
Present-day studies insist
hydrogen wasn't to blame for the disaster, rather,

the fault lay within the ship's skin.

By the time the Hindenburg approached the landing site
it had assumed the electrical potential
of the atmospheric layers it came from.
Ship and ground were on the same electrical potential,
but not so for the outer shroud. Voltage shifted

from ship and ground to frame and shroud.

Tension between parts of a poorly conductive shroud
resulted in the electrostatic discharge
which set the shroud on fire.

No way to save the ship when lift cells started burning.
See, Helen? Even if the thing were fat with helium it would've blown,
if the outer shroud's construction stayed the same.

Desperate to save face, Hitler called the explosion
an Act of God.

Shadow cutter cutting
two-headed lovers

✤

Smogless days, I see asylum dwellers
from our balcony.
Jules tells me I'm staring too much

I'll turn into one of them. Patients lie like figurines
in the grass, once in a while
someone rolls over.

Jules glances across rooftops toward 999,
kisses my wrist, scratches his head,
returns to his capsules in the bathtub.

At dusk, a crone cuts shadows near the brick wall,
an old blue-lipped sphinx who won't let us pass
till she shades us.

She motions us to stand back to back.
Hands us our shadow made with scissors
and craft paper.

Lanterns illuminate
a sunset's green flash and the garden path
leading to the asylum doors.

Our profile is a janiform head.

Curator's Scrawl: Steady white light dead ahead

✣

Helen enough about airfare let's talk
warfare

give them a panel recounting the Great War
and the first zeppelin raid on London,

those mammoth balloons, bomb-breasted
grotesque goddesses, those

height climbers with black
underbellies arriving over pitch dark England,
smelling out cities like runts from a litter, those

babykillers flying back to Germany before dawn.

British pilots never captured the fleets gristling
with machine guns, too high and swift-footed,

till faster planes and smarter weaponry
exacted phosphorous-laced revenge,
sending hot fire through demon skins

zeppelins burning the night sky like Phaeton

and suddenly airship warfare days were over,
Germans forced to transport people not
bombs.

Preacher in leather
tap shoes

✤

One block north of 999 on the corner preaching
in a weathered lab coat and leather tap shoes.

The Man in White opens the bible
randomly:

and a mighty angel took up a stone like a great millstone and cast it into the sea,
saying, this with violence shall that great city Babylon be thrown down,
and shall be found no more at all

each day on my way to the museum
he points his long crooked finger at me:

the first angel sounded, and there followed hail and fire mingled with blood,
and they were cast upon the earth: and the third part of trees was burnt up,
and all green grass was burnt up

Revelation: Jules didn't kiss me
this morning. Or yesterday or the day
before.

Still, these trailing blistered arms grope
for predawn light.

Curator's Scrawl: sun symbol black anvil crawler

✤

Here's Hitler, Helen! Draft us
a screamer from this:

First comes the USA 1927 Control Act:
Nobody gets bulk use of helium from now on
but our own government, tough luck shout the Americans.

So we'll inflate the LZ 129 with volatile
Hydrogen! Retort the Germans.

Then, to stay afloat during the depression
the Zeppelin company accepts whacks of money
from the National Socialist Party

who emblazoned swastikas on the ship's fins.
Ancient sun symbol into anvil crawlers,
sky spiders

dropping Third Reich pamphlets
over Germany, commanding media
to call the ship LZ 129.

Propaganda trips: Berlin 1936 Olympics,
Nuremberg Nazi party convention
and political rallies in empty zeppelin hangars
holding tens of thousands of hitlerites.

In her brief career she evoked wonder (dreamboat body),
dread (fins).

A great hit in America, seducing crowds and media,
nearly all crossings sold out.
Flew regularly back and forth between Germany and New Jersey.

Enviable on-time record, soft quiet ride, luxurious
and safe (other countries had abandoned airship-building
due to numerous scorching mishaps).

When she finally crashed and burnt
the Nazis insisted the world wouldn't be left
remembering German failure,

urging the Zeppelin program onward
until the outbreak of World War II.

Undertaking

other projects, Germany finally dismantled
all remaining zeppelins.

Ether eyes
m e

✣

The more I'm immersed
in the phallic floating deathship the more I desire

sex. Every day now.

("it gives me strange feelings" said a passenger
aboard the Hindenburg)

Lovemaking takes a spin not so gentle, more
biting scratching bleeding
sucking

— what's going on Helen, your face lit up like a jack-'o-lantern, eyes
and mouth ablaze these ripe red lips

Jules' chalk-white mime hands
devour me.

Passion, cut to look like a human face,
has turned me to flammable liquids.

Non-rigid: soft. Blimps. Nothing but balloons
with engines, shaped by pressure

Semi-rigid: getting bigger, harder. Solid metal keel; hybrid
between non-rigid and rigid

Rigid: always hard. Zeppelins. Solid, covered framework
equipped with numerous cells

blimps and semi-rigids emptied of gas
collapse like rags.

Jules falls away into an etherized sleep.
From our window the upper regions are black tonight,
burning planets veiled by a shroud.

✤ II ✤
Flamebirds

Ghost time our turn
to burn

✤

Lighter than air we died blazing
through ether,

limbo ghosts wandering from fire to fire around
past burns, future burns, now burns (Jules and Helen loveburns)
we're airships specters shattered by violent storms,
broken by sky crashing into hillsides and seas colliding
with power lines

eventually drifting
to the biggest most luxurious flameboat.

In the best accommodations, floating
across the Atlantic and when our zeppelin lights up
we explode from the ship like phoenixes

renewed.

Lakehurst is our favorite hearse we'll always come back here,
torched before the Hindenburg and after, we know

what happens to Jules and to Helen, see
the feather lamp blazing, Jules crouching in a corner
drinking something clear as hydrogen,
howling at the reddening sun like a loup garou.

So hang on to your skyhorse.
Ignite.

Forward thrust
and lift

✤

May 3, 1936: liftoff at 14:17 hrs
(our ride lasts 77 hrs 8 minutes until May 6 Day of Ascension,
40 days after Easter Sunday on the Holy Day of Obligation at 19:25 hrs
we are falling
slowly).

In the world's largest aircraft we rise
from Friederichshaffe, Germany
heading toward Lakehurst, New Jersey.

Jules runs the sculpting awl lightly along Helen's backbone

We are itching aching burning
for this aerial experience, unaware at takeoff
that our flight has begun, ground leaves us
motionless

Helen presses her face against the bedroom's brick wall, smells soil then rain

minutes in the air: motors turned on.
Slight incline we ascend
higher

skinned, they drop to the floor, awl rolls under the bed taps the brass
        post then chimes

with a gas capacity of over seven million feet,
strong enough to lift a gross weight of seven
elephants

Helen holds her breath, old glass wounds throbbing in her palms

length : 803.8 feet, width: 135.1 feet
empty weight: 118 tonnes, service
weight : 220 tonnes
total gas capacity: 7,062,100 cubic feet, lifting
gas type: hydrogen

Helen feels splinters in her back from the hardwood floor

propulsion: 4 propellors, diesel Mercedes Benz engines
fuel: 88 m 3 diesel in barrels, additional 4500 lubricant in barrels
range: 8,000 miles, maximum speed: 84.4 mph

Jules moans then slides off Helen, brushing an eyelash from her lip,
      which he'll coat

passengers: 36, crew: 61
Atlantic crossing time: 60 hours westbound 50 hours eastbound
1936 Airfare: $400 one way, $720 round trip (price of a brand
new car)

her soul slips into this man like a fly into amber
framework: duraluminum ribcage, cells
coated with gelatin solution to ensure against
permeability of hydrogen

no not his tears it's only sweat from his temples like glycerine semicolons

outer shroud: heavy and light cotton, heavy
and light linen. Impregnation: five layers
of a cellon paint with aluminum, plus basic layer of iron oxide.

Ship shape: cigar, phallus, or Jules' sculpture
of a Waterman fountainpen.

**Sun sets scarecrow
fields ablaze**

⚜

Sequins and boas waltzing

across an observation deck, dancing shadows cast
through barren farmer's fields: before burning
we glide through rural Germany.

Cruising along 80 knots, recordplayer
near the ship's open windows airing Madame Butterfly.

To hysterical dogs five hundred feet below,
we toss bones and diamond-studded
slippers

the ship terrifies horses and hens.
Cows and sheep don't notice us.

Funny feeling, sailing through sky
like angels or

satyrs, we can't not think about the form of the ship
and lovers to be had while on board

things kept falling, farmers said afterwards and,
*them rich folk drifted by so quiet, but for the
distant melody like a mermaid song . . .*

*went home to make babies, most days
the zeppelin floated past.*

Stay in bed watch the sea through your window

✤

Carried inside smooth lines of a ribcage,
earth passing below then ocean

we eclipse the whale

but our cabins are small (78 x 66 inches), outfitted
with upper and lower berth, folding basin,
collapsible table and signal to call attendants.

In the lounge, a mural traces the course
of explorers who rose then fell.
Gemsoaked hands take turns at an aluminum
baby grand piano, covered with soft pigskin.

In the reading room we compose letters
on unique Hindenburg stationery:

Dear Abigaile,

*You should have come life is ~~slight~~ light
up here,*

love Hal

Next door, an ashtray full of blazing embers.
How dangerous, how odd! A smoking room
in an airship filled with hydrogen!

The airtight asbestos-lined lounge contains a sole
lighter, secured with cord—
before boarding ship all matches were removed from us,

the little gold thing the only source of flame
available on the ship.

For now that is.

Meanwhile look through the porthole
(always time for eavesdropping between
card games), see Jules chastising Helen
for wanting to make love

— what's wrong with you Jules, it's been weeks
— nothing sorry I just can't
— but there's no blood
— it's the thought of red
— the *thought* are you insane! What're you looking at out there?
— geese in the asylum park
— want to go for a walk?
— no not up to it. I don't get it, they only practice, that flock
— practice?
— never actually migrate. Make their sky formations and land in the park
    again
I've watched for years, they've never left that green square more than a
    couple hours

– I thought birds died if they didn't migrate
– they'd die if they broke the flight pattern habit so they repeat
        their aerial shows, going noplace
– what about a movie?
– no. Damned birds. Feels like they're watching me
– dinner?
– no Helen don't want to do anything I'm tired

Ladies and Gentlemen Jules has turned
into a white-livered lover
and autumn so colourless for Helen,
trees without orange or red only one

maple in the yard whose purplish leaves
remain stubbornly hooked to their branches,
small bruises.

Sic itur ad astra
(Virgil: this way the road to the stars)

✣

Unmanned airballs of canvas and paper,
heated by fire on the ground. The year is 1783
and baffled audiences watch the first living creatures
carried into sky:

rooster, duck and sheep.

From now on men float
around the countryside. Peasants,
frightened out of their minds
beg priests to run for bells, books and candles
to exorcise the bloated demons above.

We crash and start fires in their fields.

Better results with your cutlass or shotgun,
says priest.

Soon we reject being carried by the wind,
wanting to steer our flight but how? Let's harness
great eagles to the gondola or build a fish-shaped balloon
to influence direction!

With sails, rudders, fins and oars
we conquer cloudbanks, rowing through air
a few seconds before colliding or igniting

. . . His aerial costume consisted of a robe of oiled silk
lined with white fur, his waistcoat and breeches in one of white satin
quilted, and morocco boots and a Montero cap of leopard skin . . .

burnt beautifully, this technicolour bird.

There goes another
sculpture

✤

Want to know what we saw, want to hear
about the lovers quarrel? Jules coating
the tyrian perfume flask, we watched
for months till the blob took on a dirigeable's shape, then Jules
painted **The Helen** along the little ship's body, in German blackletter
and who should smash the sculpture against the wall, that's right,
Helen told Jules he'd gone too far, cruel joke,
she threw the sculpture across the bedroom, unaware of the content
till the piñata exploded and fireworks of sparkling slivers
landed on the carpet and Helen gasped and Jules
bit his hands.

Land and sea swell below, we feast on fine food and wine

�֍

Birdseye view from the dining area, near
a promenade's slanted windows.

The following provisions are necessary for a round trip:

5500 pounds of fresh meat and poultry
220 pounds of fish
330 pounds of delicatessen items
800 eggs
220 pounds of butter
220 pounds of cheese and marmalade
55 gallons of mineral water
33 gallons of milk

An endless supply of the best reds and whites,
pâtes à la reine, carmen salad, indian swallow
nest soup, beef broth with marrow
dumplings, fresh black forest brook trout, cold
rhine salmon with spiced sauce and potato salad, roast
gosling meunière, fattened Bavarian-style duckling,
venison cutlets beauval with berny potatoes, tenderloin
steak with goose liver sauce, château potatoes and green beans
à la princesse, iced california melon, pears condé
with chocolate sauce, Turkish coffee, cakes and liqueurs and champagne.

Odd, eating birds as others
glide past us.

— Helen no more reds I can't eat this take the sauce off the table,
only cream sauces from now on
— Jesus Jules it's freezing in here I just want to warm up,
at least turn the heat on
— no, too hot and Helen I'm begging you, take off the red
nailpolish.

Men stand fountainpens on tables and make wagers during meals,
betting their pens won't fall over during the ride.

Sun Rise:
— Morning love want some coffee hey that sculpture is really coming along
is it another ice floe, zeppelins sailed over the arctic did you know?
Bleach, what for? Okay on my way home, bye.

Trial then error time
to pull out

&

Dreamship Log Entry, Count Ferdinand Von Zeppelin, April 23, 1874:

Basic Idea: a big ship, rigid circular and longitudinal ribs.
18 separate gas cells. Cloth covered hull.
Shape: like the body of a bird; dynamic propulsion foreseen,
machine placement and space for cargo, mail, packages
and passengers under the ship's body.

In an enormous floating arc
anchored on lake Bodensee, a crazy count spends years
hidden away with his band of builders.

July 2, 1900, the people of Friedrichshafen, Germany,
witness the maiden voyage of the LZI
(L as in *luft*, German for air; Z for the inventor).
The first rigid airship ever flown boasts an aluminum frame,
sturdy enough to coast through tempests without

folding in on itself.
A steam launch chugs toward the hangar,
pauses, groans before slowly pulling
out

exhaling
a colossal cigar-shaped ship.

The new design is the perfect military scout tool!
Count Zeppelin's dreams come true
when his vehicle becomes the world's first strategic bomber.

Liftoff.
Pale, these skeletons constructed around bags of lifting gas.

— You sure you have to go the whole week?
— if I want to sell anything, yes
— next time I'll join you, you go so often now if I didn't know any better
I'd think you were having—
— sure, next time
— well at least it's only Montreal not the arctic, call when you get there
— it'll be late I'll call tomor-
— tonight
— better go
— alright love, have a good
flight.

Air
mail

✤

Helen darling,

Pay attention, you don't even know your name means sun from Helios,
naked god on that old museum urn you're staring at,
bright shining one, ship-launching face
that started a ten year war so pay attention, Jules sees

Hell in your name, casting shadows
on his blank canvas.

Yours,
Flamebirds

PS what's that wrapped around your neck
looks like an old parachute patch you should start wearing
colour again.

We are your votive
candles flickering

✤

In the lounge smokes a handsome pilot,
twisting his dark moustache.

One foggy morning in 1945, this disoriented firestarter flew
his bomber into the 79th floor of the Empire State Building.
The Japs are bombing New York with V-2's!
cried observers.

14 perish, Empire State reopens
for business two days later.

Spaceshuttle embers also glint around our ship.
Won't get trapped inside this time, no returning

to 1986, bright blue January day when a failed "O" ring
caused an explosion
seventy three seconds after takeoff, orbiter cockpit
shearing off and crashing,
astronauts inside.

None of us dare ask
if they perished right away

or experienced the horror of descent until impact.

We should have seen it by now. It should be here by now . . .
seven more disintegrate
entering the earth's atmosphere.

We all have descent horrors, us height climbers.
Keep them to ourselves.

What does NASA stand for?
Need Another Seven Astronauts.

Take off his shoe, see
a god's extraordinary talon

✤

Here comes the Goodyear blimp, here comes

a dark feather sandal tattooed on a pale fin, here comes
the winged foot of Hermes, god guiding travellers
along their way, god of flight hired by Hades
to conduct dying souls to the underworld

here comes the god of stones, cairns and boundaries
and phallic monuments set up at crossroads, pale
as miniature blimps, called *herms*.

At sunrise, the Goodyear blimp
floats across the Toronto skyline like a shark.

Today, Helen won't think of Hermes' soft boot,
but of stone cold herms as she stares
at her feathered lamp.

Now a major motion picture starring George C Scott and Anne Bancroft

❖

Silver pens upright on the lounge table,
our fence for a house of cards we're watching
Helen and Anna watch the ship's
trip on TV

Airing tonight, motion picture Hollywood classic
The Hindenburg.

A "Jesus not Hitler" banner flashes across the screen,
live footage clips flicker to handsome actors.

— You can't be serious, Jules thinks the Man in White is after him?
— talks about going north all the time now says they won't find him there,
says he loves me. Weeps on my lap. Vanishes awhile.
My tendons hurt there's a burning
-quit drinking vodka the burning will stop did I tell you we have a new
    renter, teaches painting works with oils and bright colours, smears it
    all over the place, handsome man you'd like him I'll bring him to
    your opening
— don't know what more I can do don't you dare Anna I still love Jules
— but Jules is spiraling down dear.
Christ these clips make my skin crawl, did your museum really paint
swastikas on the fins?
— hell no they suspended the beast at the entrance in all its purity
— well I agree with Melville too much white's abnormal it's the airship's
    albinism

I dislike, same for the albino squirrels living near you
in the asylum gardens.
— hmm. So what was your favourite part?
— easy. Storm scene when lightning strikes the ship staticking the insides
and his lady friend says "next time let's take a boat, *daahhhlllinnng.*"

Tongue twist: in a cloud clipping ship we sip champagne

✦

Two dull days of staring at sea,
six hours behind course due to tempests.
Still, the captain lets us circle New York awhile

waiting out gusty winds, heavy rain
3 PM: floating above Times Square then Wall Street,
peppered grey with silk suits.

Drifting past sightseers on the West side of Broadway
while from rooftops, sidewalks and fire escapes
thousands crane their necks to watch us pass.

Airplanes escort us, buzzing around our body
like hornets. Ship and skyscraper sirens scream
in greeting.

We stop street traffic, drivers leave their cars,
some wave with delight, others stand
horrorstricken we are a UFO we are the enemy
airship.

Hovering above the Empire State:
photographers await our arrival beneath the silver peak
designed as a dirigible mast long ago,
then never used.

Gliding past the Museum of Natural History, past the Hall
of Ocean Life where a great blue whale suspends
from skylight by a single thread.

Light beams illuminate our swastikas.
It is 1936. People are unbothered by the old
sun-symbol, mark of Phaeton's forefathers.

Skyscrapers appear below like columns of staples.
Viaducts and highways thin as paperclips,
the Statue of Liberty small as a dreidel.

After rounding the Lady of the Harbour
we cross over Ebbet's Field in Brooklyn
where the Dodgers are playing the Pirates.

The game pauses for fans to stare but wait—

above the Skydome now,
where Jules and Helen watch the Jays against the Yankees.

Our swastikas wash away like a fugitive watercolour,
passing above the lovers we don another label: ATTO
in large black letters, casting
a long shadow across millions in sunsoaked bleachers.

— Jules, that word ATTO, what is it?
— insurance company I think
— reminds me of something else don't know why
— Warriors of Islam
— what?

Floating away from Jules and Helen, passing above the asylum.
Patients peacefully reading clouds in the garden until
we are spotted.

Silent Doom Harbinger, they become hysterical.
Hollering, jumping, shrieking, running toward brick walls
weeping laughing what
                                        demon is this?

Only the Man in White stands in his chalk circle,
calmly observing, an albino squirrel hopping frantically
around his tap shoes like Hitler's brain.

From deep within the folds
let the spider lines down

✤

It's taken 77 hours 8 minutes
to arrive at this point. Finally
we turn south toward New Jersey.

3:35 : BROKEN CUMULUS CLOUDS SURFACE
WIND SOUTHEAST 11 KNOTS GUSTS 20 KNOTS
SURFACE TEMPERATURE 74 PRESSURE 29.63 FALLING
SLOWLY AR.

When do we get down? I'm tired of cruising around.

4:00 CROSSING OVER LAKEHURST RIDING
OUT STORM

Meanwhile Helen scribbles the climax
of man's dream to conquer air:

The Graf went around the world without mishap, carrying over 1,300 passengers
from Germany to Brazil, through the Arctic and over the lonely planes of Siberia.
When after 7,000 miles the zeppelin arrived in Tokyo, a national holiday was called.

Hovering safely above the rain,
tea and sandwiches served.

5:35 WE WILL WAIT YOUR REPORT
THAT LANDING CONDITIONS ARE BETTER

13 hours late when a Helios beam cuts through stormclouds,
gilding our gondola windows.

6:22 CONDITIONS DEFINITELY IMPROVED, RECOMMEND
EARLIEST
POSSIBLE LANDING

all engines idle ahead, releasing
1,100 pounds of water before drifting to a dead
calm stop.

Drop the steel spider cables astern,
twilight is early.

Encore: let curtains fall
then cut the rafter ropes

✤

Lovers standing beneath the opera house chandelier,
crystal spiders dangling. One Last Date.

Time's almost up, almost our turn
to burn

then rise from the pyre drifting
around other passions,

fickle spectres smelling out new torch songs.

(Should've played Flamebird Ex Machina
from the start, extinguishing this aria
sooner).

Opening night sponsored by LORD
cultural resources

❧

6:25: Helen in gown avoiding crowds,
sneaking to the marine life chamber:

Among the Inuit there are taboos concerning the killing
of the white whale, as it is believed that the shade stays within the body for four days.
The whale symbolizes the allegorical sea-monster: its shape is the world and its mouth,
the grave that concealed Jonah then disgorged him three days later.

Her text, composed years ago, fades on the azure wall
beside an egg tempura whale.

Adjusting her hairclip, applying lipstick
then joining Anna in the photo gallery.

— Congrats, great writing
— see these walls?
— redder than a Bergman flic
— used to be an astronomy display here, they painted over millions of stars

Guests sip wine and scan horror-stricken faces of survivors:
men in suits running from wreckage, people on fire jumping from windows,
blazing bodies crawling in sand

a videotape hooked to a colossal monitor
replays the explosion on a reel.

— Where's Jules tonight?
— not coming, don't know

— cruel man, yours. Show me the ending label?

Pushing through the crowd, toward the golden dome

Like the albatross, a bird that once dominated the sky,
these giant airships could no longer reign except as ghosts
in dim museums and between dusty pages of old books.

— how clever, geez you're obsessed with that bird

A clown on stilts lunges toward the women
tossing museum brochures at masses, diving
back and forth beneath the dome.
A barbershop quartet tunes up on stage.

7:15 PM: *That All Men May Know His Work.*

Clown detaches his legs, jumps
into the control car, sticks out a purple tongue
setting the crowd into wild applause.

Acrobats juggle flaming bowling pins,
quartet singing faster no longer in unison

— well *this* isn't what I expected
— a circus?
— read my mind seen enough let's go.

Herb Morrison of WLS Radio, Chicago reporting from Lakehurst

❀

Tonight, the world experiences its first tragedy
where radio and film media are eyewitnesses.

Well here it comes, ladies and gentlemen, we're out now,
outside of the hangar . . . it's a marvelous sight. It's coming down
out of the sky pointed directly towards us and toward the mooring mast.
The mighty diesel motors just roared, the propellers biting
into the air and throwing it back into a gale-like
whirlpool . . .

Ghost time, our turn to burn (Jules, I'm home you there?)

. . . the sun is striking the windows of the observation deck, on
the eastward side, and flashing like glittering jewels on a
background of black velvet. And every now and then the
propellers are caught in the rays of the sun their highly
polished surfaces reflect surfaces of gold. The field that
we thought active when we first arrived has turned into a
moving mass of cooperative action. The landing crews have
rushed to their posts and spots, and orders are being passed
along, and last-minute preparations are being completed, for
the moment we have waited for so long.

Blazing through ether (Hungry, love? I'll make you something to eat)

The ship is ridin' majestically toward us, like some great
feather. Riding as though it is mighty good—mighty proud
of the place it's claimed in the world's aviation. The ship
is no doubt bustling with activity, frequency, orders are
being shouted to the crew, the passengers are probably
lining the windows looking down and ahead of them,
getting a glimpse of the mooring mast . . .

hang onto your skyhorse (Jules?)

It's practically standing still now, they've dropped ropes
out of the nose of the ship, and it's been taken ahold of
down on the field by a number of men. It's starting to rain
again, the rain had slacked up a little bit, the back motors
of the ship are just holding it just enough to keep it
from—

7:25 PM: high on the port side
of cell five, just above the swastika a flutter
in the skin fabric

— what's that smell Helen I told you I can't tolerate
strong odours anymo—

Faint reddish jack-'o-lantern glow

✤

—it burst into flame! It burst into flame and it's
falling, it's fire, watch it, watch it, get out of the way,
get out of the way, get this Charley, get this Charley, it's
fire and it's rising, it's rising terrible, oh my god what
do I see? it's burning-bursting into flame, and it's falling
on the mooring mast and all of the folks agree that this is
terrible, this is one of the worst catastrophes in the
world, ohh the flames are rising, oh, four or five hundred
feet into the sky. It's a terrific crash ladies and
gentlemen, the smoke and it's flames now and the frame is
crashing to the ground, not quite to the mooring mast, all
the humanity, and all the passengers. Screaming around me,
I'm so—I can't even talk, the people, it's not fair,
it's—it's—oh! I can't talk, ladies and gentleman,
honest, it's a flaming mass of smoking wreckage, and
everybody can hardly breathe . . . I'm concentrating. Lady, I'm
sorry, honestly, I can hardly breathe, I'm going to step
inside where I cannot see it. Charley that's terrible. I, I
can't . . . listen folks I'm going to have to stop for a
minute, just because I've lost my voice, this is the worst
thing I've ever witnessed . . .

– burning my sculptures quick Helen water bring water
your lamp my capsules!
– Jesus calm down move out of the way Jules move, just
a few damaged, look at me don't be so cold it was an accident,

wait where you going there's a storm it's freezing outside take your—

slam.

. . . then came a dull thump, like the sound of a gas stove lighting.

Eye witness accounts
of flaming birds

✢

07:25: At 260 feet our ship jumps forward in the sky
we explode

tail sinking to ground swastikas ablaze
we burn, fire spreads up the hull, burning though the belly
to the nose, burning in the front end of the ship

I saw one guy jump from the nose, but it was too high and he got killed,
when the nose hit the ground, I saw a second guy, he walked out of the nose,
without a stitch of clothing on him except for his shoes. All burned off. He died right
there.

Our blazing control car bounces off the ground,
comes to rest on the Lakehurst field, we burn.

In 37 seconds, 7 million cubic feet of hydrogen
torches our ship

I saw people blown out the windows, then it started falling,
very slowly. Pieces were coming down like snow.

62 survivors, mostly window jumpers
running to escape the blazing fireball.

Ironical ending twist: in recognition of his heroism,
Lakehurst personnel present a cigarette case
to the severely burned captain to replace the one he lost
on board.

Captain dies in hospital.

Germans honour 36 of us in funerals
with a sinister straight-armed salute.

In the passenger compartment, one old couple sitting on the bunk,
didn't even know what happened.
Walked out of the blazing ship, unscratched.

❖ III ❖
Into Thin Air

Abort
ship

✱

Little love demon slips out of me, tired
fire

bleeding onto the berber carpet.
Jules has vanished

into thin air.

Last moments, after the blazing feather lamp
is extinguished:

cooling my face against our frosted kitchen window,
cheekbone melting a circle in the ice through which,
minutes later, a lone dark smudge treks through the blizzard.

Jules wiping soot off his sculptures then struggling to tie
his shoelaces, shaking, a diamond of pale skin showing
between the pant leg and the sock.

This pale diamond is what I remember most.

He walked out the door and I thought
to myself,

that skin flap will die
from frostbite.

Back in the glass studio

❧

— What's wrong Anna you're flushed

— glass master went back to his ex-wife in Prague. I'm deflated like your
   blimp, ha

— so why continue taking up with old marrieds?

— because they shatter me but first they teach me to blow. Here, brought
   you a snake

— Medusa?

— started falling off one by one before he left

— looks like fulgurite lightning

— fulgurite nothing it's a swizzle stick. Besides, now that all her hair's fallen
   out, I realize Medusa looks better bald. Think Jules'll return?

— did. I was working. Left ten half-burnt sculptures and a dusty book

— which book?

— love letters between F. Scott and Zelda Fitzgerald

— burnt trapped in an asylum, didn't she?

— don't know haven't reached the end yet

— smash the sculptures?

— empty

— NOTHING inside you're telling me all this time he's been putting
   thousands of coats on not a goddamn thing?

— all but the roman flask, only one I watched him paint

— and your relics swiped for art?

— saw the Man in White yesterday. Wearing my cameo.

Stared past me and asked, "ever met your life?"

looked behind then up and there was the Metropolitan Life Insurance
blimp floating by, red baron snoopy cartoon on the nose,

demanding, HAVE YOU MET LIFE TODAY.

So I know it. Arctic or Montreal or

— the madhouse is where he's headed Helen

— or Montreal and someone else, he's

gone.

Rest
in pieces

❧

Unhooked from the golden dome, replaced
with a tin submarine.

The new exhibit is called,
"Mission Accomplished: two thousand leagues under."

I narrate stories of torpedo technology, Poseidon missiles
and a deep submergence vehicle called *Trieste*.

The exhibit will feature a simulation of a nuclear fast attack
submarine control room complete with periscopes,
ship and ballast panels, multiple sound effects.

"The kids'll love this one!"
bellows the Museum Director.

The dismantled Hindenburg rests
in the cold storage vault
with arctic furs and stuffed white creatures,

in a tightly sealed crate
beneath a shelf of albatross wings.

Supermarket tabloid headline:
It was Venus not an Airship

✤

Wasn't a UFO it was lava-drenched lovestar Venus
shamelessly shining near the sun, dark beauty
spotted glinting near the horizon

no alien vessel just cupid's mom
tossing rocks from the heaven-vault

comets defrosting their ice heads on fireballs
spinning brightly

burning down,
love.

~~Post~~ Ghost Script

⚜

70 miles from the center of New York City,
come to our crash site.

Take the New Jersey turnpike to Garden State Parkway South,
to Exit 88. Follow Route 70 West, take a right at the Gulf station
then left down the 547, ¼ mile to the gate.

The Lakehurst motel flashes a neon blue blimp.
See the Naval Air Center and the Air Ship Bar next door?

The gate guard will give you a special Hindenburg Pass
for the dashboard. You're probably the only visitor.

A miniature zeppelin windvane on a rusty pole
marks the crash spot, and a plaque lying flat in the sand.
Dusty plastic wreaths in a field of asphalt and weeds.

Wait for the wind then get a shot of the small zeppelin
with the enormous hangar as backdrop (original still standing,
replica control car from 1975 motion picture inside).

The Lakehurst Historical Society Museum
is open three hours on Wednesdays and Sundays.
Artifacts include ground crew badges, serving platters,
girder and rope, silver spoons.

The annual memorial service takes place May 6th at 7:25 PM, commemorating *all airship crashes throughout history.*

Since the 65th anniversary of the disaster
the air base is closed to the public, except
for pre-booked tours.

Visit the site from outside the gates,
look up!

See one last spectacular airshow
before government rebuilds on the land.

These birds, my flaps
of skin

❖

Sit crosslegged like the scribe
weigh my heart against a feather.

Past the timberline. Farther north
than where nests the albatross.

A cold white thought took you long ago

to a place where it hasn't rained in a million years
and stones are shaped by air, not water
but sky.

Air galleons higher, row
skyward

lover, this way, this way the road
is this way what's that up there

burning?

❖ ❖ ❖

Acknowledgements

Information about the Hindenburg and the history of Zeppelins comes mainly from M. Mooney's *The Hindenburg*, New York: Dodd, Mead & Company, 1972; M. Flynn's *The Great Airships: the tragedies and triumphs: from the Hindenburg to Cargo carriers of the new millenium*, London: Carlton, 1999; W. Althoff's *Sky Ships: a history of the airship in the United States Navy*, California: Pacifica Press, 1998; and the Navy Lakehurst Historical Society's official website.

The citation on page 14 is from the Royal Ontario Museum's rotunda entrance, where the words *That all men may know his work* are inscribed in the middle of the dome's mosaic ceiling.

Citations on page 30 are from the Book of Revelations, 18:21 and 8:7 respectively. Information about ballooning and the citation on page 47 come from the article, "When Man First Left the Earth," *Horizon*, September 1958 vol.1 no.1: 114-128. The citation on page 51 is from the personal notebook of Count Ferdinand Von Zeppelin, obtained via world wide web. Radioed text on page 62 and 63 is from M. Mooney's *The Hindenburg*, New York: Dodd, Mead & Company, 1972: 195-197. Text from Herbert Morrison's radio broadcast transcript was obtained via world wide web and witness citations of the airship explosion on page 71 and 72 were obtained from historical newspaper clippings.

My thanks to NeWest Press for believing and to Don Kerr for his editorial guidance and insight. Thanks also to Magda Khordoc. Et Daniel, for unfailingly putting up with the writer in me. Finally, to my family—pater for tracking down those books, marms for patiently rereading first drafts and sis for the encouragement, the jokes, and for always listening.

NINA BERKHOUT was born and raised in Calgary, Alberta, where she earned a degree in Classical Studies at the University of Calgary. After completing an MA in Museum Studies at the University of Toronto, Berkhout moved to a remote island in the Bahamas to set up a community museum-the setting for her first collection of poetry, *Letters from Deadman's Cay* (NeWest Press). Berkhout currently lives in Winnipeg, where she works as a historical researcher. Nina Berkhout is also a poetry reader for *Contemporary Verse (CV2) Magazine.*